IMAGES
of America

St. Johns and the North Portland Peninsula

Capt. Meriwether Lewis and Capt. William Clark's Corps of Discovery journeyed to the Pacific coast. On the way back, Captain Clark, his slave York, a Native American member of his group, and others ventured onto the Willamette River from the Columbia in 1806 and camped near an abandoned village. Some say this crew made it as far as the land below the University of Portland, or even further. (Author's collection.)

On the Cover: The St. Johns Bridge is pictured under construction, possibly in late 1930. It was designed by engineers David B. Steinman and Holton D. Robinson of New York. Several construction firms were utilized. Construction began on September 3, 1929, and the bridge was dedicated on June 13, 1931. (Author's collection.)

IMAGES
of America

ST. JOHNS AND THE NORTH PORTLAND PENINSULA

Donald R. Nelson

ARCADIA
PUBLISHING

ISBN 978-1-4671-0505-7

Published by Arcadia Publishing
Charleston, South Carolina

Printed in the United States of America

Library of Congress Control Number: 2019954264

For all general information, please contact Arcadia Publishing:
Telephone 843-853-2070
Fax 843-853-0044
E-mail sales@arcadiapublishing.com
For customer service and orders:
Toll-Free 1-888-313-2665

Visit us on the Internet at www.arcadiapublishing.com

For my wife, Patty.

Contents

ACKNOWLEDGMENTS

In memoriam—in this past year, Edna Harvey, Sharon Helgerson, and Joan Brown, all members of the St. Johns Heritage Society, went to their heavenly home. Henry E. Rassi, a valuable historical source, also passed away in 2019.

I would like to thank Tom Stubblefield and Stuart Johnson, who spent many hours informing me about St. Johns history when I started my education about St. Johns in 2011. Alan Toelle, a Gatton descendant, has shared his extensive family research over the past several years. Kathy Baker-Katz and Wilma Fineberg sent me several photographs pertaining to their families in St. Johns. Thanks to the Shackleton, Rassi, and Patterson families for their assistance. Thanks to Gil Parton, an enthusiastic accumulator of St. Johns history, who scanned much of the St. Johns Heritage Society collection of images and provided me with the fruits of his labor.

There are many—too many—for me to attempt to mention each contributor by name, but I do thank them for the shared memories and photographs over the years.

Please note that North Lombard Street was originally Jersey Street; the name was changed in 1959. Lombard Street is the name used throughout this book. Oregon Historical Society will go by the abbreviation of OHS.

Introduction

My interest in St. Johns resulted from a conversation in 2011 with Neña Rawdah, owner of St. Johns Booksellers. She suggested I look into the history of the community for a book project. This led to many conversations with descendants of early-day families who have shared their memories and photographs over the years.

This title for Arcadia Publishing continues the St. Johns story while adding more of the North Portland Peninsula to the mix as well as many newly found old photographs. Recent conversations with area residents have helped to chronicle the ongoing changes. The following pages are but a sampling of the past. There is still much to be uncovered and documented.

Native Americans populated the land in and around St. Johns in the early 1800s. Explorers Lewis and Clark and their Corps of Discovery were dispatched by Pres. Thomas Jefferson to document species of animals and plants and to find passage on the Columbia River to the Pacific Ocean. Their mission began in 1804. They did not reach Oregon until 1805. After reaching the ocean, the decision was made in 1806 to go down the Willamette River, which they had missed earlier. William Clark, his slave York, a Native American pilot, and others stopped for the night near an abandoned Native American camp near Gatton Slough. Some accounts say they went as far down the river as below today's University of Portland.

Pioneers filed for donation land claims beginning in the 1840s. St. Johns was annexed to Portland in 1891. Taxation issues led to St. Johns seceding from the city in 1895. Apparently, it was not documented in the records; the Oregon legislature finally put it in the books in October 1898.

It was a sleepy village without much industrial development in the late 1890s. A barrel factory was established in 1865 and was the main industry for nearly 30 years. The company owner was St. Johns's first postmaster in 1873.

The Port of Portland was established in 1891 to maintain a shipping channel from the mouth of the Columbia River to the Willamette River. The organization installed a dry dock in 1904 for ship repair and later an airport at Swan Island in 1927.

Many blue-collar industrial developments occurred in the early 1900s. Railroad development in 1902 along the St. Johns waterfront led to sawmills and other industries.

St. Johns incorporated in 1903 and established its own city government. A city hall was completed in 1907. Taxation within the city rose to such heights that the citizens voted to be annexed to Portland again.

Nearly every denomination established churches in St. Johns. Education was important too.

Shipyards thrived in the late 1910s, as ships were produced for World War I.

The St. Johns Bridge, planned for several years just before the Depression, was completed and dedicated in 1931.

Many brick business blocks were erected. When Prohibition was lifted in 1933, combined beer parlors (taverns) and card rooms began operating in St. Johns.

Although St. Johns suffered through the Depression of the 1930s, life went on.

Shipyards were also built in and near St. Johns in the war years of the 1940s, revitalizing the community with jobs. The Housing Authority of Portland built residential areas in St. Johns.

The St. Johns Plaza was built in 1979 and a clock was installed. It was part of a revitalization plan by the city of Portland. It is a gathering place for events and a waiting area for the buses that traverse the community.

Nearby University Park is home to the University of Portland (UP). It is a Roman Catholic university that was established as Columbia University in 1901 on the former site of the Methodist operated Portland University. Columbia Preparatory school (Columbia Prep), a high school that had strong academic and athletic programs, was also located on the UP campus for many years.

The ebb and flow of history, combined with the human experience, has brought forth an ever-changing narrative of the development of St. Johns and the surrounding areas.

In the past few years, many long-established businesses have closed, and many longtime residents who were history resources have passed away.

Old buildings and houses have been dismantled to make way for new housing opportunities to reach density objectives. The city of Portland continues to grow. The St. Johns community in North Portland is growing with an influx of new residents.

St. Johns is a tightly knit, independent community today, as it has always been.

One

In the Early Days

The lighthouse at the confluence of the Columbia and Willamette Rivers was designed by architect Carl W. Leick, who worked for the 13th Lighthouse District of the US Lighthouse Board. The lighthouse in this c. 1901 photograph was built in 1895 and was in use for another 40 years. (Author's collection.)

James John first lived in Linnton before establishing himself in St. Johns with a 320-acre donation land claim in 1846. He then platted the land in the early 1850s, which was recorded in Multnomah County in 1865. He operated a ferry from St. Johns to Linnton and built a house and a store at the foot of North Burlington Avenue. Alice Severance Learned recalled in the mid-1920s that James John was a peculiar character. He was nicknamed by his neighbors "St. John." Because the plat was misnamed St. Johns instead of St. John, the post office was named St. Johns when it was established. (Painting ©Mike Noce.)

St. Johns historian David Swart wrote in the *St. Johns Review* that John "always identified himself as Jimmy John and was known in his later years as 'Demijohn.' John was a quiet person, generous to a fault, resisting invasion of his privacy, modest of his exploits. And educated far beyond the average person of his day." James John was known to get along better with children than their parents. He left his estate to provide for the education of the children of St. Johns. This is a painting of his store based on a c. 1902 photograph. (Painting by author.)

Lewis Love, a pioneer of North Portland, sits at a table for a formal portrait. In 1850, he and his wife established a donation land claim of over 630 acres on the Columbia Slough. The land extended south, east, and west of the slough. Love was a farmer, built steamboats, and was involved in various real estate holdings in Portland. After a full life, he passed away in 1903. (Courtesy St. Johns Heritage Society.)

Lewis Love is buried in the historic Columbian Cemetery, a property that he donated for cemetery use. His grave is shown in this 2011 photograph. (Photograph by author.)

William Gatton and his wife, Nancy, came to St. Johns in 1852 and settled on a 320-acre donation land claim that they farmed. Today, Terminal 4 occupies a portion of their claim. Later, William purchased over 300 acres. This family portrait dates to around 1865. They had eleven children; six lived into adulthood. Nancy died in 1871. (Courtesy Gatton descendants.)

William Gatton (left) and his brother Samuel pose for their photograph in the late 1860s. Samuel lived in Washington Territory at the time. (Courtesy Gatton descendants.)

The beginnings of Terminal 4 (left center) on the former William Gatton land are seen in this c. 1918 photograph. (Courtesy Alan Toelle.)

This 1920s grouping of buildings was part of the William Gatton farm. This view was photographed when the farm was rented by the Widmer family, who had rented the farm in the early 1910s. The house was moved in the 1940s and survives today, greatly remodeled. The hill that it was on was leveled for industrial development. (Courtesy Alan Toelle and Widmer family.)

The Oregon Barrel Company is seen in this c. 1890 photograph. The business was on the waterfront of St. Johns between North Charleston and North Richmond Avenues. Benjamin O. Severance started the business in 1865 as Pacific Barrel Company. They made sugar barrels as well as barrels for pork, fish, and liquor. The sugar barrel staves were sent to Hawaii, filled, and sent back. Eventually, the sugar companies began putting their sugar in sacks. The Oregon Barrel Company then shifted to making woodenware. After Severance's death in 1903, the machinery was put to other uses. (Courtesy Severance and Learned descendants.)

Men stand in front of a building at the Oregon Barrel Factory. A flag flies above. Severance was the postmaster from its beginning in 1873 until 1891. His daughter Alice Learned was the assistant postmaster to him for most of the time that he held the position. (Courtesy Severance and Learned descendants.)

Benjamin O. Severance posed for this formal portrait in the 1890s. (Courtesy Severance and Learned descendants.)

The extended family of Benjamin and Mary Severance enjoys a family gathering around 1890. At left in the front row are, from left to right, Alice Vicera Learned (daughter of Benjamin O. Severance), her husband Albert Frank Learned (an employee of Severance), and their son Otis (next to the dog). At right are Benjamin O. Severance and his wife, Mary. (Courtesy Severance and Learned descendants.)

Amos L. Miner and his wife, Sarah, came to St. Johns in the mid-1880s. He bought 57 acres. He was a farmer and developed some of his land into a housing addition. They had come from Minneapolis, Minnesota, originally. He was involved in real estate and business. His farmhouse, on the left in this 1894 photograph, stands today on North Syracuse Street. (Courtesy OHS)

A woman with a bouquet of flowers stands on a promontory overlooking the North Portland Peninsula, where St. Johns is located. The Columbia River is in the background and the Willamette River is in the foreground of this c. 1910 image. Beyond the bow on her hat is Sitton School. (Author's collection.)

Two

Growth and Businesses

St. Johns was a separate community until it was annexed to the city of East Portland in 1891. East Portland, the city of Albina, and the west side city of Portland consolidated later that year to become known as Portland. St. Johns was incorporated in 1903 after seceding from the city of Portland in the 1890s because of taxation issues. The landmark St. Johns City Hall building was built in 1906–1907 at the intersection of North Philadelphia and Burlington Avenues. It also housed the police and fire departments. The sign on the railing in this c. 1908 photograph reads, "Vote here for City and County." The structure was built with bricks manufactured in St Johns. (Author's collection.)

At left in this c. 1904 photograph is a City & Suburban streetcar at North Lombard Street. The two-story building at left was built as Bickner's Hall. It was a community gathering place on the second floor, a place for meetings and theatrical performances, and the original location for St. Johns Christian Church. The structure later became the McGill family's St. Johns Hardware Store. The top floor was removed around 1930. All the buildings to the right of it were torn down and replaced. (Courtesy OHS, BB0084011.)

North Lombard Street is being graded in this 1905 photograph. Central School is on the left. The site is occupied today by the James John School playground at North John Avenue. Streetcar tracks are seen angling from the lower left. (Courtesy OHS, Org. Lot 1390.)

North Leavitt Avenue is being graded between North Ivanhoe Street and Syracuse in 1907. The house at center was occupied by Michele and Maria Noce and their children in the 1920s. Noce family descendants lived there into the late 1960s. (Courtesy OHS, Org. Lot 1390.)

This is a drawing of a float for the Spirit of the Golden West parade, which was a part of the 1908 Rose Festival. It depicts the prosperity envisioned for St. Johns, which was then a separate city. The bridge has striking similarities to the St. Johns Bridge, which was built 22 years later. St. Johns, annexed to the city in 1915, has never come close to this depicted grandeur. (Author's collection.)

This c. 1910 view shows the Marine Iron Works, which was later known as American Iron Works. It was located at the foot of North Richmond Avenue. The products manufactured there were, according to a 1908 advertisement, oil and water tanks, marine and stationary boilers, hydraulic pipe, and sheet iron works. (Courtesy Gholston collection.)

The Western Cooperage Company is under construction in this c. 1914 photograph. It operated until the late 1950s. (Courtesy Stephen Kenney.)

When the Spokane, Portland & Seattle Bridge was completed in 1908, it was said to be the longest draw span in the world. The swing span was replaced by a horizontal lift section in 1988 because the bridge was considered a hazard for ships to pass through the draw. It is now known as the Burlington Northern Santa Fe Railroad Bridge 5.1. The image above is from around 1908, and the one below is from 2011. (Above, courtesy Stephen Kenney; below, photograph by the author.)

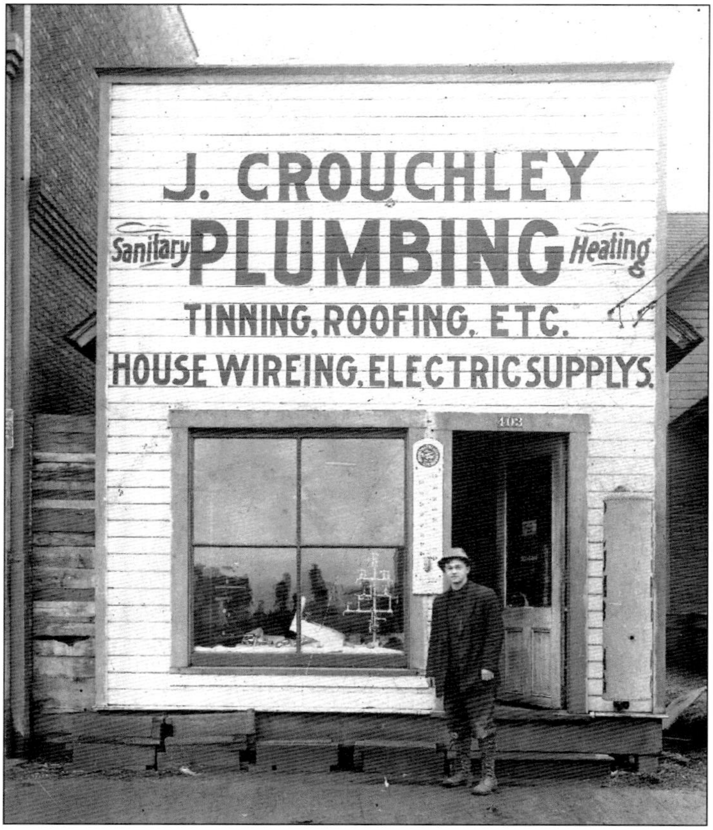

The J. Crouchley Plumbing Company was established around 1906. It was located next to the Leo Building on North Lombard Street and North Chicago Avenue, as seen in this c. 1910 photograph. Ernest Crouchley, brother of Roy, stands in front of their building. (Courtesy Crouchley family.)

Pictured is the interior of Crouchley Plumbing around 1910. James Crouchley is seated; Earl Crouchley is next to the stove. (Courtesy Crouchley family.)

The Central Hotel, built around 1904, was in the Cochran Block for many years. The balcony on the building gives it an old west appearance; it was later removed. The Surber & Cochran card room and beer parlor later occupied most of the first floor. A grocery store, the St. Johns Cash Grocery, occupied the corner at North Philadelphia Avenue and North Lombard Street for many years. The upper floors were removed in 1939 due to poor conditions. (Courtesy St. Johns Heritage Society.)

Eventually, the bar became known as Dad's, then Brad's, before it was renamed the Central Hotel. The Central Hotel at North Philadelphia and North Lombard Streets, a restaurant/bar, was demolished in late 2018. It was to be rebuilt as a boutique hotel with three stories, as it originally stood, but the plans did not come to fruition. A new structure has been planned for the site. (Photograph by author.)

The St. Johns Hotel at North Baltimore Avenue and North Ivanhoe Street opened in April 1906. An advertisement in the *St. Johns Review* stated that "This new and up-to-the hour hostelry will be finely equipped in every way. Rooms may now be booked. Cuisine will be excellent. Grill-room and bar connected with the hotel." The structure still stands, greatly remodeled, and is now named the Sentry Building. (Courtesy OHS, Org. Lot 1390.)

The Port of Portland dry dock, as seen in this c. 1910 photograph, was built in 1094 and was later enlarged. The dry docks were moved to Swan Island in 1953. (Courtesy Severance and Learned descendants.)

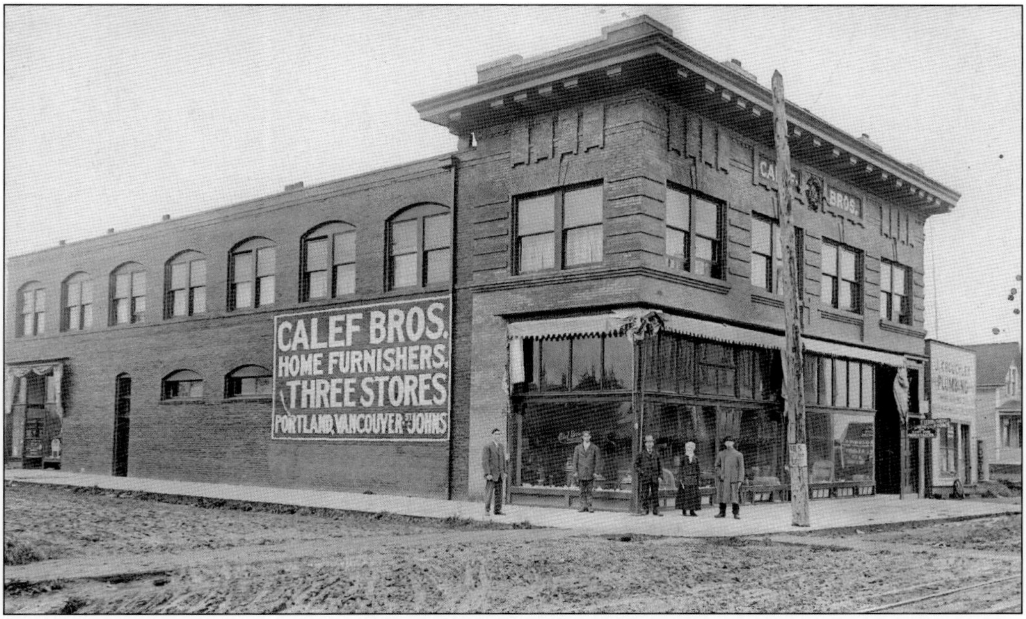

Dr. C. Gee Wo (Chequong Gee Leo Wo), who was also listed in Portland City directories as Gee Wo Leo, was a practitioner of herbal medicine in Portland for many years. He advertised his remedies in local newspapers. Wo erected a brick building on North Lombard Street and North Chicago Avenue in 1906 named the Leo Block. Calef Bros. Furniture was the original storefront tenant. Furnished rooms were available on the second floor. Crouchley Plumbing was in the wood frame building next door to the north. (Above, courtesy Stephen Kenney; below, author's collection.)

WHY DO YOU SUFFER?

When the Great Chinese Doctor

C. GEE WO

can cure you of any ailment by his powerful and harmless Chinese herbs and roots, which are unknown to medical science of this country. His wonderful cures throughout the U. S. alone tell the story. Thousands of people are thankful to him for saving their lives from OPERATIONS

Then why let yourself suffer? This famous doctor knows the action of over 500 different remedies that he has successfully used in different diseases.

The following Testimonials from well-known people tell of the wonderful curative powers of nature's own herbs and roots:

Thomas Walsh, Tenth and Everett street, City, cured of stomach trouble two years' standing.

Miss Helene Enberg, 506 Vancouver avenue, city, suffered many years with dyspepsia of the stomach and lung trouble, and was said by doctors to have incurable consumption. I am thankful to say, after five months' treatment of Dr. C. Gee Wo's remedies, I have fully regained my health and strength. I recommend all that are sick to go and see him.

Saved from operation: Mrs. Theresa George, 705 Fourth street, city—I had suffered from inflammation of the womb and ovaries and female weakness, and tried many doctors, but all said I would die if I did not have an operation. I tried Dr. C. Gee Wo's remedies as my last resource, and am thankful to say that after four months' treatment I was entirely cured.

He guarantees to cure Catarrh, Asthma, Liver, Kidney, Lung Trouble, Rheumatism, Nervousness, Stomach, Female Trouble and all private diseases. Hundreds of testimonials. Charges moderate. If you are sick with any of the above ailments then call and see him. Consultation free. Patients out of the city write for blank and circulars. Inclose stamp. Address

The C. Gee Wo Medicine Co. 253 Alder St., Cor. 3rd
Portland, Oregon

Wan Jower operated a men's and women's clothing store on the west side of Portland beginning in the 1880s. When rents were too high, he built a store in St. Johns in 1906. Jower and his family are posed outside of their building in the c. 1910 photograph above. They had five boys who worked at the store at various times. They also had a daughter who died young. Concerns were raised about the quality of the Jower building construction when it was first built. In the mid-1970s, George and Marilyn Korenaga bought the business and remodeled the exterior. Many came to Jower's to buy their work boots and clothing. After 100 years in operation, Marilyn decided it was the appropriate time to close the store. The Jower building was completely redesigned and renovated in 2017. (Above, courtesy Marilyn Korenaga; below, photograph by author.)

Alex S. Scales built a grocery store in the Cedar Park area on North Fessenden Street around 1906. He was in business with his brother Norman for a time. His brother John owned the store when it was sold to Oliver Balke in 1911. It was then operated as Balke & Cowles (his father-in-law). The store and its inventory were sold to Alex Scales in 1913. The store was in operation by Scales until the late 1910s. L.K. Simmons owned the store from about 1920 until 1927. It was later known as the St. Louis Feed Market in 1948. This part of Fessenden was renamed St. Louis Street in the early 1930s. Advertisements and Simmons's name were still visible on the structure in 2011. Vacant for many years, it was torn down in 2018. (Above, courtesy Sandy Ball; below, photograph by author.)

In 1909, the (Alex) Scales & (Upshur) Curty grocery store was built on North Fessenden Street, North Columbia Way, and North Oregonian Street. Thomas Scales, father of Alex, operated a real estate office next door. Alex Scales bought out his business partner in 1910. Richard Scales took over the store. He later partnered in a grocery store with Edmond Currier. (Courtesy Sandy Ball.)

In the mid-1930s, Scales once again operated a grocery store out of his original building on Fessenden. He started selling beer to his friends, who played cards after hours. He eventually turned his establishment into a combined grocery store/beer parlor named the Six Point Inn. The business was sold in the 1940s. He later operated Jack & Jerry's Tavern at 5903 North Lombard Street. (Courtesy Sandy Ball.)

In 2015, the Six Point Inn was renovated and renamed Over Easy Bar and Breakfast. This photograph is from 2018. (Photograph by author.)

George W. Roberts and his wife, Myrtle, had a combined grocery, confectionery, and filling station at North Willamette Boulevard and North Edgewater Avenue. An advertisement for White Clover ice cream is on the porch of the building in this 1920s photograph. In 1938, it was under new management and was named Portway Grocery. By 1944, the Portway Grocery was listed as a grocery and beer parlor, later becoming the Portway Tavern. (Courtesy Portway Tavern.)

This c. 1908 view shows the Stine Block at the corner of North Lombard Street and North Burlington Avenue. The Bonham and Currier Department Store, after being located elsewhere, moved into the Stine Block in 1907. They offered hollowware (such as metal tableware), groceries, clothing, and other products. (Courtesy OHS, Org. Lot 1390.)

The Stine Block was remodeled in the late 1930s. Starbucks, a longtime occupant of the building, closed its doors in 2019. (Courtesy Jim Staub.)

The S.W. Simmons livery stable, seen here around 1900, stood at the corner of North Richmond Avenue and North Syracuse Street. (Courtesy St. Johns Heritage Society.)

This c. 1910 view of St. Johns was likely photographed from a water tower. St. Johns City Hall is seen at upper left. The dark building at right center is the S.W. Simmons livery stable. (Author's collection.)

Dr. Joseph McChesney built the McChesney Block, in the right background, around 1910. This photograph dates to 1911, when North Lombard Street was being paved. This view is looking from North Chicago Avenue. The McChesney Block was home to the St. Johns Post Office for over 20 years. (Author's collection.)

Dr. Joseph McChesney and his wife came to St. Johns around 1905. McChesney built a residence on North Willamette Boulevard and North Chicago Avenue in 1908, which still stands today. He continued to practice medicine until a few days before his death in 1944. The photograph was taken around 1911. (Author's collection.)

The St. Johns Library opened in 1913 when the community was its own separate city. The library operates as a branch of Portland's Multnomah County Library. It is located on North Charleston Avenue, north of North Lombard Street. (Courtesy Stephen Kenney.)

In the 1914 *Polk's Portland City Directory*, the Central cigar store was listed under "Billiard Parlors." It was located in the Central Hotel. Norman I. White operated the Central pool parlor in the same structure in 1916. The pool parlor was located on North Philadelphia Avenue between North Ivanhoe and North Lombard Streets. (Author's collection.)

The Grabeteria, a clerk-less grocery store on North Lombard Street, moved to a new two-story structure in 1923. The grocery was operated by Edmonde S. Currier of Bonham & Currier (B&C), and Fred Couch, son of early merchant K.C. Couch. Currier retained ties to his former company, which he co-founded around 1905. He and Couch bought the Grabeteria in 1918, and the grocery operations of B&C were phased out. The former grocery store is occupied by St. Johns Vision Clinic. There are offices above. (Courtesy OHS, org. lot 1390.)

The First National Bank of St. Johns is decorated with patriotic bunting in honor of the Benevolent Protective Order of Elks convention in Portland in June 1912. The bank opened in 1908. The structure was later renamed the Peninsula Security building and also contained the Peninsula Mortgage company. Offices were located above. Today, 45th Parallel Wines occupies the lower floor. (Courtesy OHS, Org. Lot 1390.)

St. Johns finally had a first-class movie theater in 1911. A few years later, it was showing four-reel shows, which changed daily, a feat not accomplished by many theaters at that time. Several years ago, Ethel McGill recalls that when she was young, she went to the silent movies with her older brother. Title cards contained the dialogue. Since she was not old enough to know how to read, her brother read the cards to her. Peninsula Recreation was put in the former Multnomah Theatre in 1935. It had a two-lane bowling alley, beer parlor, and seating on the main floor. An upstairs balcony, reached via a spiral staircase, contained a lady's parlor and seats for spectators. The building on North Lombard Street was later home to Goodwill and today is occupied by a store named Therapy. (Above, courtesy St. Johns Heritage Society; below, photograph by author.)

Couch & Company was a general merchandise store on North Philadelphia Avenue between North Syracuse and North Ivanhoe Streets. This view is from around 1916. K.C. Couch, the proprietor, was twice elected mayor of St. Johns. He had also been the president of the St. Johns Commercial Club. By 1938, the St. Johns Lumber Company operated from this location. (Author's collection.)

By 1962, Carl's Union Service Station occupied the former site of Couch & Company. This 1989 photograph shows that the service station was closed. The restaurant Our Daily Bread can be seen in the background. The building had previously been used as a Pioneer Pie restaurant. (Photograph by author.)

The apartment house Marvel 29 was built in 2013 on the former site of Pioneer Pie and the service station. (Photograph by author.)

This 1938 photograph is of the Firemen's Pond in front of the St. Johns City Hall. It was built by off-duty firemen in the early 1930s and featured a bridge, ponds, and an American Flyer electric train, which would run on Sundays. It was a favorite place to gather on the weekends. The pond, which had been unused since the 1950s, was removed in the mid-1960s. The lumber company in the background is today the site of the Marvel 29 apartment house. (Author's collection.)

Business partners in the St. Johns hardware store Charles S. McGill and William R. Evens built this automobile building on North Jersey (Lombard) Street and North John Avenue in 1920. Peninsula Motor Sales briefly occupied this building in 1920, followed by Fields Motor Car Company from 1920 to 1922. Raymond Fisher operated his Chevrolet dealership and garage after that for many years. By 1933, it was home to the Bachelors' Club Arena, where boxing and wrestling matches were held. (Courtesy McGill family.)

StormBreaker Brewing–St. Johns opened its brewpub in St. Johns in 2018. It is located in the former Bachelors' Club Arena, which later was utilized for doctor's and dentist's offices. It is located at North Lombard Street and North John Avenue. (Photograph by author.)

Tom's Super Service Battery and Electrical Works, a full-service gas station, was at North St. Louis Avenue and North Ivanhoe Street. Tom Buckles was the proprietor. This photograph dates to around 1931. (Courtesy Portland Archives, A2009-009.2611.)

This is the Venetian Sandwich Shop around 1933, which was next door to the Venetian Theatre. Luella Hoes was the proprietor of the shop, which faced North Lombard Avenue. She was selling "the New Hamburger" for 10¢. It is now occupied by Affogato, a coffee and gelato shop. (Courtesy St. Johns Heritage Society.)

Louis Larsen was the manager of H. Matthew Pihl's St. Johns Transfer & Storage Inc. in the mid-1930s. He left the company to start his own, St. Johns Motor Express, shown here. In the foreground of this 1930s photograph is the firemen's pond, which was built in front of the St. Johns City Hall. The fire station was then located in the city hall. (Author's collection.)

After Larsen left St. Johns Transfer & Storage, Lenore Pihl, wife of H. Matthew Pihl, attended business courses at the request of her husband so she could become the manager of the company. She was affectionately referred to as the "Mother Trucker." She is seen with the company trucks in this c. 1938 photograph at James John Elementary School. (Courtesy Hollie Pihl.)

This 1939 view shows the St. Johns waterfront; on the left is the Portland Woolen Mills. The structure at center was built in 1930 for the Hood River Canning Company. For many years, it was occupied by Columbia Sportswear. Moonstruck Chocolate, the current occupant of the structure, has been in the building since 2002. A portion of Peninsula Iron Works can be seen on the right. (Author's collection.)

This is the St. Johns Funeral Home at North Ivanhoe Street and North Leavitt Avenue around 1941. It was at one time occupied by mortician A.L. "Dodd" Berg. Hustad's Funeral Home was located here until 1958. This corner is now part of the US National Bank parking lot. (Courtesy Mike Noce.)

Chiropractic physician Dr. Carlton Mast stands outside his new building in 1940 on North Charleston Avenue, north of North Lombard Street. He began his practice in St. Johns in 1924. Dr. Mast retired in 1966. (Courtesy St. Johns Heritage Society.)

Messiah Lutheran Church, a Finnish congregation, purchased Mast's building in 1981 and added a second floor for use as a sanctuary. The church, pictured in 2011, was sold and demolished for future development. (Photograph by author.)

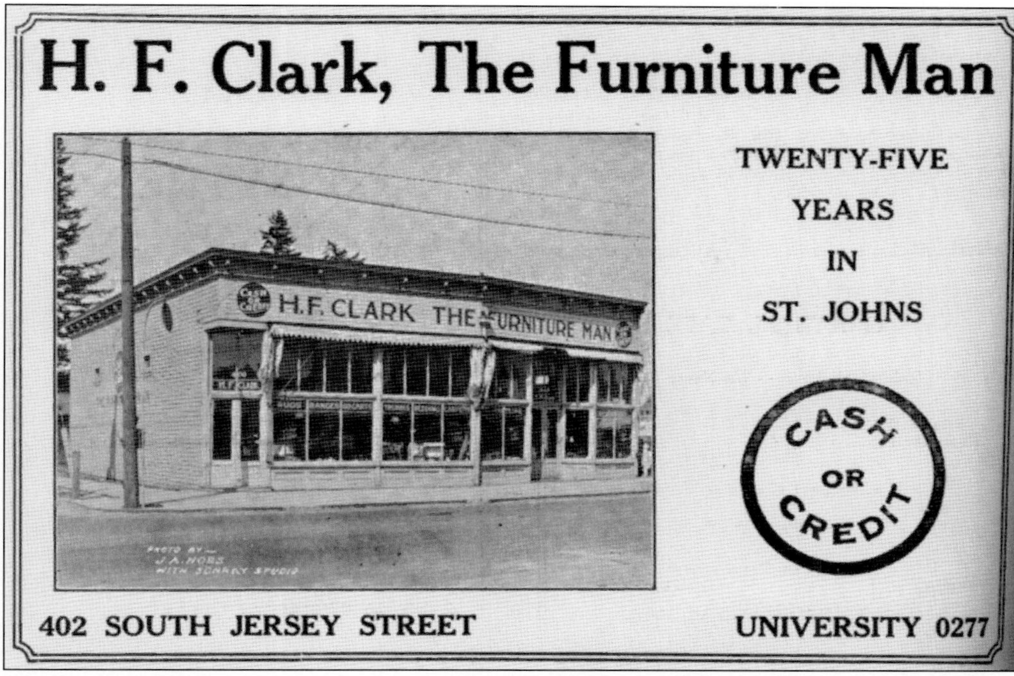

H.F. Clark, "the Furniture Man," was located in this building at North Lombard Street and North Charleston Avenue for several decades. This view is from 1931. Weir's Cyclery later occupied this structure. (Courtesy *St. Johns Review.*)

The Union at St. Johns apartment house was built in 2018 on the former site of Weir's Cyclery and the Messiah Lutheran Church. (Photograph by author.)

Portland Woolen Mills, located along North Burlington Avenue, was built in 1904–1905 and closed in 1960. Owen Shackleton remembers, "Portland Woolen Mill was a very important mill in St. Johns, and they made blankets." He saw a unique sight from the bridge in the 1940s. Depending upon what color the blanket they were making, the dye used was turned loose in the sewer system, and the Willamette River would turn blue or green or other colors temporarily. This photograph was taken around 1944. (Courtesy St. Johns Heritage Society.)

Pictured is the Portland Woolen Mills cafeteria, lunchroom, and clubhouse around 1919. It was still standing in 1976, a total of 16 years after the business closed. It was last used as the company recreation hall and mill ends store, according to a 1976 newspaper account. (Author's collection.)

Daniel S. Duff, in the dark suit at center in the first row, was the superintendent of the new St. Johns Post Office on North Ivanhoe Street between North Alta and North Baltimore Avenues. He poses with the first group of letter carriers in front of the new post office in 1933. The post office relocated to another location in the 1980s. The Bahá'í Faith Center has been in the former post office for many years. (Courtesy St. Johns Heritage Society.)

The United States National Bank Peninsula Branch sign pierces the dark, as does The Man's Shop and other businesses in this c. 1956 photograph. In 1905, the branch was originally the Peninsula National Bank of St. Johns. After annexation in 1915, St. Johns was dropped from the title and was replaced by Portland. Two years later, the bank consolidated with the First National Bank of St. Johns, later adding the Commerce Bank of St. Johns. The bank became a branch operation when bought by the United States National Bank. (Courtesy United States National Bank Peninsula Branch.)

The Owl's Perch tavern was built at North Lombard Street near Buchanan Avenue by John "Jack" Ketrenos around 1933. His son Bob assisted him in operating it. When Jack retired, Bob continued working there. (Courtesy Bonny McInroy.)

In the 1950s, the Owl's Perch had a motorcycle club. Bob Ketrenos is third from the left. (Courtesy Fred Ryan.)

In 1952, Bob Ketrenos opened Tele Tronics across the street from the Owl's Perch. Originally televisions were sold there; eventually, it became a home furnishings store. Pictured in this 1962 photograph, from left to right, are an unidentified technician, Dorothy Jones (bookkeeper), Dick Dinsdale (sales), Lou Talariko (repairman /service manager), an unidentified Peruvian employee (sponsored by the Ketrenos family, who was a helper at Tele Tronics), and Bob Ketrenos (owner). (Courtesy Bonny McInroy.)

Bob Ketrenos, on the left, accepts keys to his new vehicles for his Tele Tronics company. These were purchased from Chevrolet dealer Fred Bauer, who is on the right in this early 1960s view. (Courtesy Bonny McInroy.)

In 1953, The Man's Shop was moving to a new location next door. They were having a "quiting" business sale; everything was for sale, including the store fixtures. All the current clothing in stock was being sold at lower prices. They relocated to the retail space to the east of the space they were vacating. (Courtesy The Man's Shop.)

This was the interior of The Man's Shop in 1960, showing the owners and employees. From left to right are Bob Leveton, unidentified, Jerry Leveton, Ben Leveton (owner), Violet Hanner, and Jean Leveton (wife of Ben and mother of Bob and Jerry). This location was formerly a Gamble's Western Auto Supply Company store. The Man's Shop closed in late December 2019. (Courtesy The Man's Shop.)

Brothers and co-owners of The Man's Shop, Bob (left) and Jerry Leveton, pose in their store in May 2018. Jerry passed away in November of that year. (Photograph by author.)

Beth Preciso (tailor) and Denny Hassler (sales) are shown in this 2018 photograph. They worked at The Man's Shop for many years. One day, mortician A.L. "Dodd" Berg came to The Man's Shop to purchase a suit. Denny, then a teenager, was the only one available to wait on Berg. When he asked the size of the suit, Berg said that it did not matter. Although a bit perplexed, Denny sold Berg a suit. It was later explained to him that the suit he sold was for a burial and that it was cut in the back to put on a body. (Photograph by author.)

Wayne E. Smith was a barber in St. Johns from 1946 to 2017. He learned his trade on the USS *California* during World War II. Among his customers were many from successive generations of the same families. When he retired at the age of 65, he cut back his work schedule to half-days. He continued working until a couple of days before his death in June 2017 at the age of 95. His shop was on North Lombard Street between North Alta and North Baltimore Avenues. This photograph was taken in 2011. (Photograph by author.)

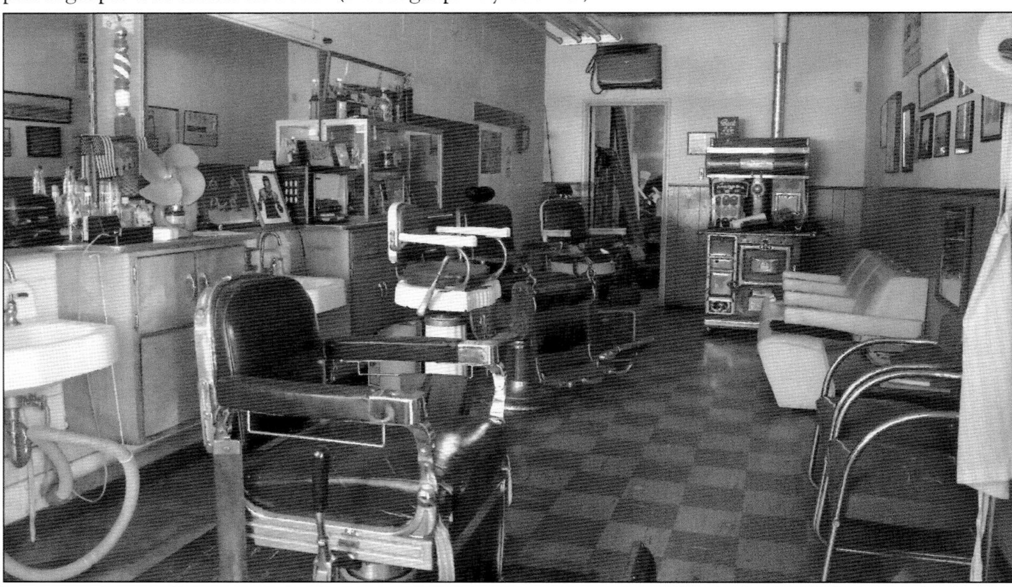

This photograph was taken in Wayne Smith's barbershop in July 2017, not long after his passing. His work apron still hangs on the coat rack. The barber supplies have been removed, but the barber chairs remain. His customers' seating area is still there. In the back is a wood stove from an early St. Johns business, Pacific Stove and Range Manufacturing Company. (Photograph by author.)

St. Johns Booksellers was opened in 1995 by Nẽna Rawdah and a business partner, who she later bought out. It was a full-service book store with book signings and poetry readings. The store, seen here in 2011, closed in January 2016. (Photograph by author.)

The Edgewater House condominium development was built in the late 1970s on the grounds of the Augustus Mortimer and Adele Stearns estate. This photograph dates to 1981; the house was built in 1910. Stearns was a dealer in timberlands and was considered one of the wealthiest individuals in St. Johns. He passed away in 1916. His wife was involved with the Young Women's Christian Association of St. Johns. She passed away in 1942. The house remains today. (Courtesy Portland Archives, A2012-008.580.19.)

Olaf "Slim" Skaug broke his legs in a workplace accident during his employment on the St. Johns Bridge when it was being built in 1930. In 1935, he opened a beer parlor and card room, which is now known as Slim's Restaurant and Lounge on North Lombard Street north of Burlington Avenue. (Both photographs by author.)

Three

SCHOOLS

The first school in St. Johns was in a log cabin; it was later replaced by a frame building constructed from wood salvaged from an old ship that ran aground. Central School came next in 1894. Sitton and George School followed. Modern buildings have replaced these buildings over the years. James John High School was built in 1910 and vacated in 1922 when Roosevelt High School was built. This c. 1884 photograph shows an early St. Johns schoolhouse on the Byars' property. Students pose with their teacher, Mrs. Skipworth. (Courtesy St. Johns Heritage Society.)

The original section of the St. Johns Central School was occupied in 1894. Several additions were added over the years. The school was later renamed the Williams School. It was due to be replaced by James Johns School. James John was nearly complete when Williams School burned on January 13, 1930; it was evacuated in one minute and 15 seconds. James John School was completed and occupied by the displaced students two days later. (Author's collection.)

A group of elementary schoolchildren, probably from the Central School, stand with picnic baskets in hand in this c. 1910 photograph. The Rose City Hotel is in the background. In the left background, near the Willamette River, is the Gillen-Chambers asbestos factory. To its left is Jobes Flour Mill; to the right is the St. Johns City Dock. (Courtesy Wilma Fineberg.)

North School, later renamed Sitton Elementary School, was built in 1907 at North Hudson Street and North Reno Avenue near Pier Park. The upper floor was used as a high school until James John High School opened in 1910. Sitton was named after Leffie Sitton, a director of the Portland School Board and widow of Portland businessman Charles E. Sitton. After being decommissioned for two years, Sitton was reopened in 1942 because of the influx of schoolchildren from shipyard workers' families. A new Sitton School opened in 1949, and the old building was later torn down. (Courtesy St. Johns Historical Society.)

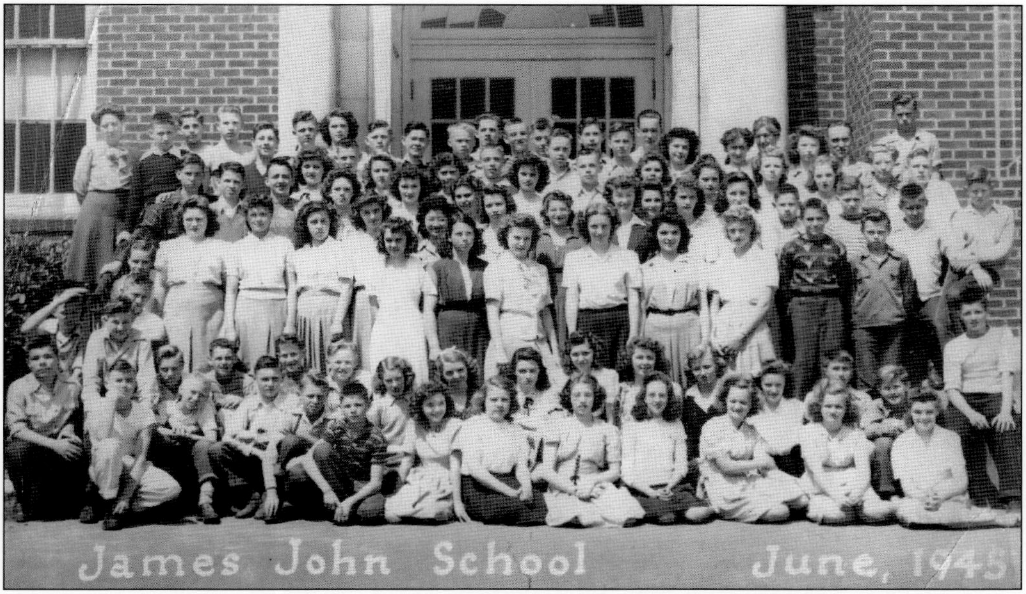

Featured is the James John Elementary School eighth-grade class in June 1945. Future St. Johns business owners Marilyn Jower and Merlin Radke are in the group. (Author's collection.)

James John High School was designed by architect Charles Burgraff of Albany, Oregon, and was completed in 1910 at North Philadelphia Avenue and Syracuse Street. In 1921, it was rebuilt due to structural deficiencies. A new high school, Roosevelt, opened in 1923. The old James Johns was then used as an elementary school until 1929; in 1934, the building burned down under suspicious circumstances. The Bridgecrest apartment complex has occupied the former site of James John High School since 1972. (Author's collection.)

This is a composite photograph of the 1927 eighth-grade class of James John School. The building was used through the 1920s. The vacant structure was destroyed by fire in 1934. (Courtesy St. Johns Heritage Society.)

George School, at North Fessenden Street and North Burr Avenue, was built in 1909. A fire in part of the school occurred in 1949, the date of the photograph. A new school was built within a year or two. The old structure was torn down in 1967. (Courtesy St. Johns Heritage Society.)

A second-grade class Christmas celebration is shown in this c. 1950 photograph in a portable building at the old George School on North Fessenden Avenue. Each student bought a gift for a dollar or two. Names were drawn, and gifts were chosen. Homemade treats were available. (Courtesy Terri Johnson.)

Henry E. Rassi was a Roosevelt High School track star in the pole vault. His highest vault was 11 feet, 2 inches. (Courtesy Henry E. Rassi.)

Students Victor Shackleton and Henry E. Rassi put on a judo demonstration during halftime of a 1947 Roosevelt High School basketball game. Here, Rassi is throwing Shackleton. There were two other events going on at the same time to entertain the spectators. (Courtesy Victor Shackleton.)

Four

CHURCHES

Local religious congregations date to the 1840s with the Methodist Episcopal Church. They were followed by Evangelical, Congregational, and Baptist organizations before the end of the 19th century. Assumption Parish began as St. Clements Catholic Church in 1911. This group of schoolchildren stands possibly on North John Avenue, north of the Willamette River. The Evangelical Church, built in 1886, is at right. (Courtesy St. Johns Heritage Society.)

A teamster pulls a wagonload of lumber past the Seventh Day Adventist Church at North Salem Avenue and Edison Street in this c. 1904 photograph. After the congregation moved to a new location, the church was rebuilt as a residence. (Courtesy OHS, BB0084013.)

The first two buildings of the First Baptist Church of St. Johns are shown in this photograph. The octagonal building was built in 1905. The one on the left, built in 1907, stood at North Leonard Street and North Chicago Avenue. (Courtesy St. Johns Heritage Society.)

The National Cash Register building, from the Lewis & Clark Centennial Exposition of 1905 in Northwest Portland, was given to the St. Johns Congregational Society after the exposition was over. It was dismantled and broken down into sections for easy transport by rail to St. Johns, where it was rebuilt at the corner of North Ivanhoe Street and North Richmond Avenue. (Courtesy Stephen Kenney.)

Later, the structure was used as a Lutheran church, an American Legion Hall, and as Duffy's Pub before being acquired by McMenamins in the late 1990s. It is now the McMenamins St. Johns Pub. (Photograph by author.)

Two women gather at the Willamette River to watch the baptism of young women from the St. Johns Christian Church in 1919. (Courtesy St. Johns Christian Church.)

The parish originally named St. Clements was located on North Smith Street when established by Archbishop Alexander Christie in 1909. It was renamed the Church of the Assumption of the Blessed Virgin Mary in 1917. The church building was dedicated in 1927. It came to be known as Assumption Parish. The three-acre site once held a rectory, parish school, and sister's school. They were relocated to other properties and became housing. An assisted living facility was built on the property and opened in the early 2000s. The church remains. (Courtesy Archives of the Sisters of the Holy Names of Jesus and Mary, US–Ontario Province.)

A new St. Johns Christian Church was built in 1955. The land had been presented to the church 10 years earlier by Dr. D.S. Swart. It is located at North Richmond Avenue and North Central Street. (Courtesy St. Johns Christian Church.)

St. Johns Methodist Episcopal Church was at North Leavitt Avenue and North Syracuse Street, as seen in this real-photo postcard postmarked 1916. The photograph probably dates to around 1910. (Courtesy Stephen Kenney.)

The St. Johns Methodist Episcopal Church is decorated for Easter in this 1908 photograph. A new building on North Charleston Avenue was built in the 1920s. It is known at Pioneer Methodist Church. (Courtesy Pioneer Methodist Church.)

Five

People, Places, and Events

The Cedar Park Picnic Grounds, shown in this c. 1898 photograph, was a park developed by the City & Suburban Street Railway Company, which had a stop at Cedar Park on North Fessenden Street. An article in the August 15, 1898, *Morning Oregonian* read, "From early morning yesterday till late in the evening those who have been unable to go to the seaside or mountains found recreation in the vicinity of the groves of St. Johns. At the end of the track is a nicely cleared grove, with platform dancing for those that enjoy that sort of amusement." (Author's collection.)

A pavilion was built at Cedar Park. The membership of the Free Methodist Church is seen in front of it in this c. 1907 photograph. The park closed around 1909. The property was developed, and many of the trees were cut down. (Courtesy Dale Burger.)

Girls of the St. Johns Christian Church are dressed in patriotic dresses, probably for a Fourth of July celebration, in the 1910s. (Courtesy St. Johns Christian Church.)

This photograph shows the St. Johns Breakers baseball club in 1907. From left to right are Harry Hunter, Charlie Brederson, Charlie Andrews, Tom Cochran, unidentified, Tom Carrol, Ben Hoover, Barney Noonan, unidentified, David Thorndyke, Lester Brink, unidentified, and Peter Autzen. (Courtesy St. Johns Heritage Society.)

Members of the Holmes Lodge No. 101 of St. Johns pose on the steps of the St. Johns Congregational Church in 1908. (Courtesy Wilma Fineberg.)

In the foreground is the ferry landing near Linnton. The St. Johns ferry is ready to make the trip to the city of St. Johns on the opposite side of the Willamette River. A steamboat ambles down the Willamette along the waterfront in this c. 1908 photograph. (Author's collection.)

The battleship *Oregon*, which saw action in the Spanish-American War in the late 1890s, sails past St. Johns in 1912 en route to its moorage location in North Portland for the Elks convention. The name Whitwood Court on the photograph refers to the location where the picture was taken. At far left is the Portland Woolen Mills. At the center-left background is James John High School. In the far-right background are the water towers of the St. Johns Water Works. (Author's collection.)

Amos Benson built his elegant home on North Crawford Street around 1910 on property overlooking the Willamette River and the Spokane, Portland & Seattle (SP&S) railroad bridge. Benson was the son of logging entrepreneur and philanthropist Simon Benson. The Edmund Chaney family occupied the house in 1924. It was sold in 1986 and turned into a drug and alcohol treatment center before being occupied by Open Meadows High School. It is now a private residence. (Courtesy Severance and Learned descendants.)

Wayfinding Academy, a two-year college, is located next to Pioneer Methodist Church on North Charleston Avenue between North Lombard and North Central Streets. The academy building was formerly the St. Johns YMCA. (Photograph by author.)

In 1923, the first year of Roosevelt High School, Lucy Lee Thomas was the school's first Rose Festival princess. She was also chosen Rose Festival Queen. This image appeared in the 1923 *Roosevelt Ranger*. (Author's collection.)

This is Walt Morey's graduation photograph from the Roosevelt High School 1926 yearbook. In the mid-1930s, he was house manager of the Venetian Theatre on North Lombard Street. Morey later wrote the book *Gentle Ben*, which was developed into a movie named *Gentle Giant* in 1967. It was also developed as a television program, which ran from 1967 to 1969. (Courtesy Portland Public Schools.)

Watchmaker Henry E. Rassi had his own shop in St. Johns. He also worked for jeweler Henry M. Tower at his North Philadelphia Avenue Shop. Rassi is seen relaxing in a hammock in the late 1920s. Exposure to radium paint for watch dials is thought to have led to his early passing at age 48 in November 1931. (Courtesy Patterson family.)

After the death of watchmaker Henry E. Rassi, his family grew flowers in their backyard. Sisters Roberta and Arlene sold them to St. Johns businesses to gain income for their family. In this 1931 photograph, Rassi's wife, Elizabeth, holds her young son Henry Jr. Her other children are, from left to right, Wayne, Robert, Arline, and Roberta. (Courtesy Patterson family.)

New street lighting was installed in St. Johns in 1926. One of the new lights was in front of the Peninsula National Bank. Currin's drugstore is next door. Dr. Watts, an eye-ear-nose-throat physician, was located on the second floor of the Peninsula bank building, which was earlier known as the Holbrook Block. (Author's collection.)

This is a scene of the St. Johns Bridge dedication parade on June 13, 1931, passing in front of St. Johns City Hall. (Courtesy St. Johns Heritage Society.)

Arline (Rassi) Patterson grew up in her family home on North Syracuse Street, not far from the St. Johns Bridge. On the day of the dedication in 1931, the seven-year-old grew tired of waiting to go across. There was to be a parade, and the band kept practicing. She ran across the bridge before the parade started. She is proud of the fact that she was the first to cross the bridge. This photograph of Arline Rassi is from the mid-1930s. (Courtesy Patterson family.)

In this c. 1942 photograph, Mike Noce is busy cleaning his tricycle at Jack's Service Station at North Leavitt Avenue and North Ivanhoe Street. Mike is the son of Gilbert Noce, who had a tailoring shop on North Lombard Street. (Courtesy Mike Noce.)

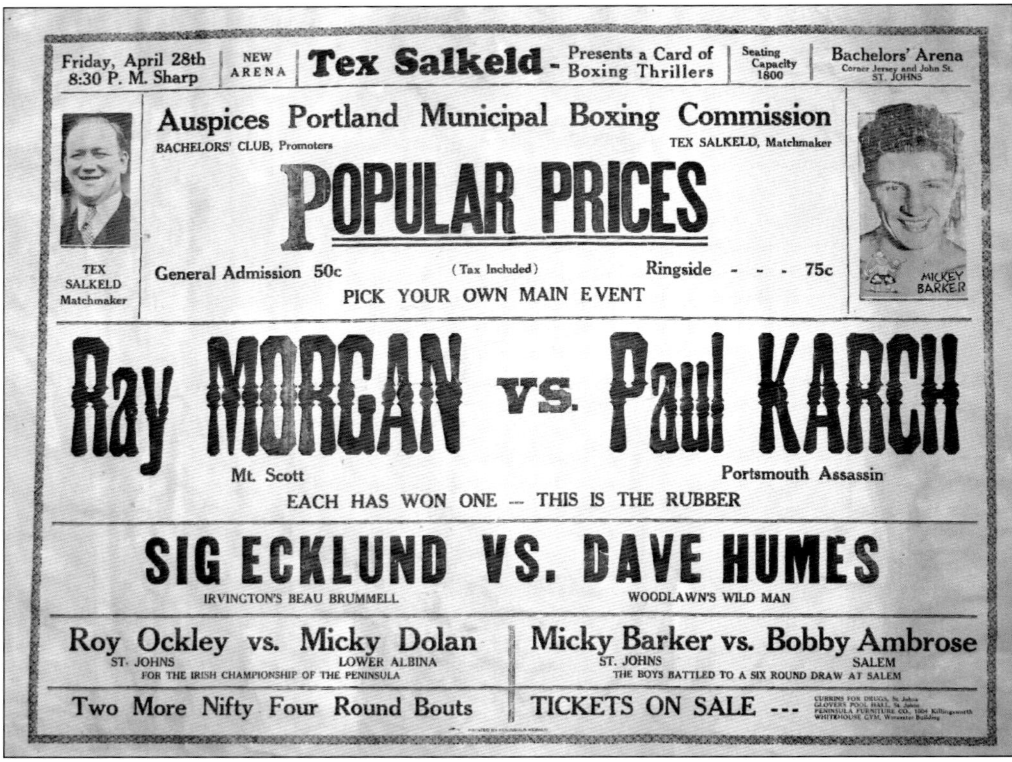

This poster advertises the boxing card at the Bachelors' Arena on Friday, April 23, 1933. It was in the building now occupied by StormBreaker Brewing–St. Johns at North Lombard Street and North John Avenue. (Author's collection.)

Carl Helgerson, from the Albina area, was a boxer in the late 1920s and 1930s. He later moved to St. Johns. These are his boxing shoes and the trophy he received for winning a Multnomah Amateur Athletic Club–sponsored boxing match at Alderwood Country Club in 1932. (Photograph by author.)

Carl Helgerson later became a longshoreman. This is a labor union–related cartoon that he drew in the mid-1930s. (Courtesy Sharon Helgerson.)

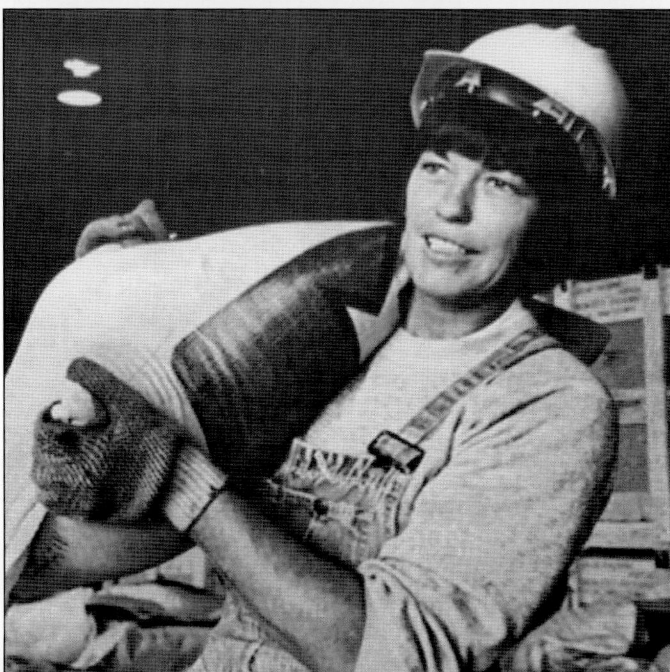

In the 1980s, Carl's daughter, Sharon Helgerson, was among the first women to work as a longshoreman in Portland. In her retirement, she was a writer who had a strong interest in preserving St. Johns History. (Courtesy Mike Brown.)

The municipal incinerator at Chimney Park is pictured in 1932. Originally used to burn garbage, it was later used to burn business papers. It closed in 1970 and the chimney was removed in 1990. (Courtesy Portland Archives A2001-062.14)

Cousins Victor (left) and Owen Shackleton (right) were mischief-makers when they were young. In one of their meanderings around the community, they made it all the way to the municipal incinerator. The sand piles they found there were enticing; they spent the whole day sliding on them. (Courtesy Victor Shackleton.)

This late 1920s photograph shows the ferry landing in St. Johns on North Pittsburg Avenue. On the left is the Rose City Flour Mill, part of which was the Gillen Cole asbestos factory. By this time, the former St. Johns City Dock had become Municipal Terminal No. 3. (Courtesy St. Johns Heritage Society.)

The Portland Basket & Handle company leased the mill property from the Portland Manufacturing Company (PMF) in 1930. PMF also made plans for an addition beyond the handle company to the waterfront. On the right of the ferry landing is the former Portland Municipal Pier No. 3. A major portion of it was removed for construction of the St. Johns Bridge. The approach to the bridge is seen in this 1935 photograph. (Courtesy Portland Archives, A2004-002.2520.)

This late 1930s photograph shows the Portland Lumber Mills structures. Wood products are on the dock, ready for shipment. (Courtesy Gene and Alana Zurbrugg.)

The St. Johns Bridge spans the Willamette River in this 1939 photograph. (Author's collection.)

This c. 1945 aerial view of St. Johns shows the Parkside Homes development at center. The gear-shaped cluster of buildings at lower right was originally a daycare for the Oregon Shipyard Corporation worker's children. Parkside Homes was built by the Housing Authority of Portland in 1942 to supply the need for housing for shipyard workers and others. The municipal incinerator is at lower left. The property with trees, around the incinerator, was known as Chimney Park. Pier Park can be seen in the left center background. (Author's collection.)

A group of friends gathers for their photograph at Parkside Homes around 1954. The identified children from the Spanke family are "T" (Terry), "J" (Jackie), and "P" (Paul). (Courtesy Mike Brown.)

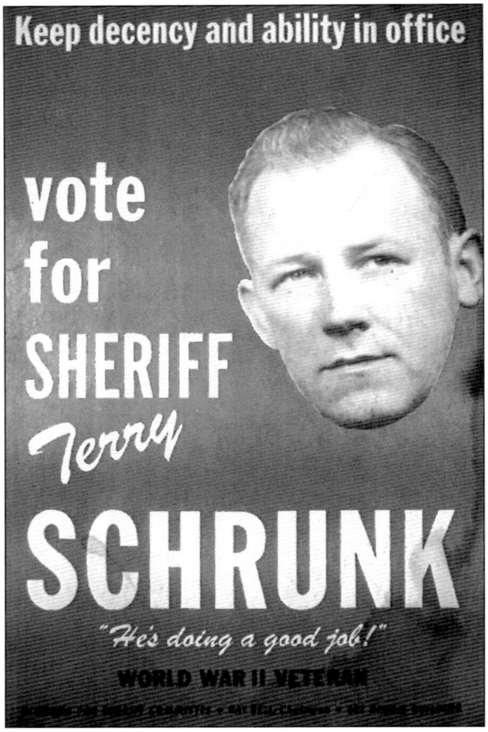

Terry Schrunk grew up in St. Johns and graduated from Roosevelt High School in the early 1930s. He was a Portland fireman from the mid-1930s until 1949, when he was appointed Multnomah County sheriff. This is a c. 1950 campaign poster for him. Schrunk was mayor of Portland from 1957 to 1972. (Author's collection.)

Pete Lulich was a recreation director at the St. Johns Community Center for over 30 years. Lulich was held in such high regard that the community center gymnasium was named "Pete's Place." He grew up in the Slabtown area of Northwest Portland. Lulich attended St. Patrick Catholic Church and played baseball at an early age. He played for Norgan's Beavers in 1945. (Courtesy Rudy Satalich.)

On the upper left of this 1947 photograph is the former housing for Oregon Shipyard Corporation workers. At upper right is a gymnasium for the shipyard, which was moved and rebuilt onto the St. Johns Community Center in 1948. (©Thomas Robinson.)

A blanket of fall leaves is on the lawn in front of the St. Johns Community Center in this 2011 photograph. (Photograph by author.)

This view looks north to the St. Johns Bridge and Willamette River waterfront in 1945. (Photograph by Rod Eggiman, courtesy Tony and Linda Smith.)

The sawmill crew at the Portland Lumber Mills is pictured in 1950. (Thomas Robinson.)

Future country music star Willie Nelson (left) and his bandmate Bobby Gibson perform at the Wishing Well restaurant in St. Johns in the mid-1950s. (Courtesy Bobby Gibson.)

Henry E. Rassi learned photography by studying the one book on the subject that the Roosevelt High School library had in its collection. In the Korean War, Sergeant Rassi was a photographer with the 1st Cavalry, 13th Signal Corps. (Courtesy Henry Rassi.)

This c. 1950 view of North Lombard Street looks toward North John Avenue. Safeway is on the left. Swanson's Meat Market, with frozen food lockers and the Super Food Mart, is to the right. At the end of the block are the offices of Dr. T.L. Staat, Dr. B.L. Phillips, and Dr. M.V. Klingler. (Courtesy St. Johns Heritage Society.)

This 2019 view of North Lombard Street looking toward North John Avenue shows a corner of the former Safeway building. Blue Moon Camera and Machine and StormBreaker Brewing–St. Johns are next door. (Photograph by author.)

In 1962, mills were still operating along the waterfront of the Willamette River. The approach to the St. Johns Bridge is on the right. (©Thomas Robinson.)

This image dates to 1978. The mills had closed a year or two earlier and were dismantled, leaving a void on the waterfront. (©Thomas Robinson.)

This c. 1965 aerial view of the North Portland Peninsula shows the outlined area of the first phase of the Rivergate industrial site. Also shown is the future expansion owned by the Leadbetter estate, which was held in trust by Willamette University and was purchased by the Port of Portland. (©Thomas Robinson.)

This is the expanded Rivergate industrial site in 1979. (©Thomas Robinson.)

This 1975 aerial view, north of the St. Johns Bridge, shows in the upper left and center the 35-acre Portland Public Automobile Terminal and the floating dock used to unload autos from ships. This dock was put in in 1970. On the right is the former Portland Woolen Mills complex, which today is Cathedral Park Place containing offices, businesses, and artist spaces. (Courtesy Portland Archives, A2010-003.)

Community activist Howard Galbraith was involved in many civic activities in St. Johns and was one of the founders of the St. Johns Heritage Society. He was part of the Cathedral Park Committee. He told his wife that he did not want a funeral: "maybe my friends will gather under the St. Johns Bridge and celebrate." The St. Johns Jazz Festival began as a celebration of Galbraith's life in 1980. The image above shows the Cathedral Park Jazz Festival in 2011. (Above, photograph by author; left, drawing by author.)

These were the management personnel of Peninsula Iron Works in 2011. From left to right are James J. Johnson (president), A.J. Johnson (engineer), David M. Johnson (vice president), Janet J. Johnson (secretary-treasurer), and Stuart B. Johnson (retired former president). (Photograph by author.)

The Peninsula Iron Works building at North Crawford Street and North Alta Avenue stands near the St. Johns Bridge. The business was founded in 1917. (Photograph by author.)

Joan Brown, a member of the St. Johns Heritage Society, holds an early portrait of herself. She was a war bride from England who came to America on the SS *Marine Flasher* in 1947. Over the years, she has been president of the Sitton School and Roosevelt High School Parent Teacher Associations. She passed away in November 2019. (Photograph by author.)

Tom Stubblefield grew up in St. Johns. As a teenager, he worked for St. Johns grocery man Odus Bales. He survived the fire in Bales's store in 1965. Bales mentored him in the grocery business, leading to Tom owning his own two stores, including one in St. Johns. He has been part of the St. Johns business community for many years, most recently owning a painting company. Among a large circle of friends and acquaintances, he is known as "the Mayor of St. Johns." (Photograph by author.)

Pattie Deitz closed her Patties Home Plate Cafe, which was located at North Lombard Street and North Leavitt Street, in November 2019 and relocated to another location in North Portland. She and her husband took over the cafe in 1998. Two other businesses were in the same structure and later closed. She absorbed the other spaces to sell a variety of items. (Both photographs by author.)

This 2019 photograph of the annual St. Johns Parade features the Roosevelt High School band. The parade occurs every May and includes autos transporting Rose Festival princesses, local school bands, decorated floats, and people from the community. Portland Civic leaders also participate. (Photograph by author.)

The St. Johns Bizarre occurs the same day as the parade. This festival includes local vendors, food, crafts, music, and the St. Johns Bizarre Biergarten, as shown in this 2019 photograph. (Photograph by author.)

Six

Transportation

Mass transit steam-powered trains began operations to St. Johns in the late 1880s. An electric streetcar line of the City and Suburban began operations in 1903. In 1937, the St. Johns streetcars, then owned by the Portland Traction Company, were replaced by electric trackless trolleys, which were busses with rubber tires powered by electricity. These electric trolleys were discontinued in St. Johns around 1958 in favor of gasoline-powered buses. Today, in Portland, busses are powered with updated fuels and technologies. According to a *Trolley Talk* magazine from 1969, steam engines pulled cars of passengers from St. Johns to Albina. This image is from around 1895. (Courtesy Peter Weiglin.)

This 1904 view of North Lombard Street features a streetcar by the Potter and Goold Hardware store. A telegraph pole is visible at North Lombard Street and North Burlington Avenue. The carbarn is at right center, where the US National Bank Peninsula Branch is located today. (Author's collection.)

R.D. Jackson's streetcar waiting room on North Lombard Street opened next door to his St. Johns Pharmacy in 1907. Cigars, magazines, ice cream (in season), as well as postcards, were offered for sale. This view shows a large bunch of bananas and a St. Johns baseball uniform hanging on the right. Three men are seated waiting for the streetcar in this c. 1907 photograph. (Courtesy St. Johns Heritage Association.)

Jitney buses competed with streetcars for several years. The signboard on this one reads St. John. This photograph dates to 1915. For several years, there were discussions about whether the town should be St. John or St. Johns. (Courtesy Jean Nixon.)

A St. Johns streetcar travels down North Lombard Street in 1916. Today, the storefronts on the left are occupied by Slim's. (Courtesy Mark Moore.)

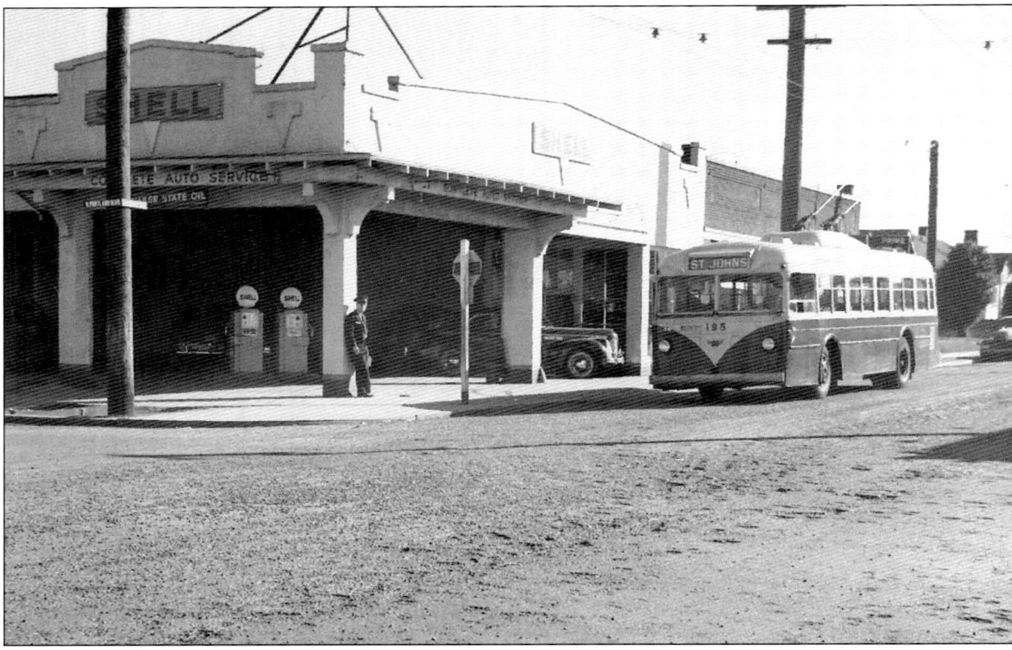

The St. Johns trolley bus is at North Rosa Parks Way and North Greeley Avenue heading to St. Johns in 1949. (Courtesy Portland Archives, A2000-025.2117.)

A Tri-Met bus is stopped on North Philadelphia Avenue near North Ivanhoe Street in 1975. The building originally occupied by Bonham and Currier is at left in the background. (Courtesy St. Johns Heritage Society.)

Seven

Shipyards and World War II

A variety of shipyards were needed to supply the ships for World Wars I and II. The Grant Porter-Smith Shipyard was located near the Portland Woolen Mill. Farther east was the Peninsula Shipbuilding Co., which was in operation before the war. Industrialist Henry J. Kaiser built shipyards for the World War II effort, the first being the Oregon Shipyard Corporation (Oregon Ship), then the Swan Island Shipyard, as well as one in Vancouver, Washington. The Grant Porter-Smith-Guthrie Shipyard was at the Willamette River waterfront west of today's St. Johns Bridge; it began operating in 1917. The name Guthrie was later dropped. (Author's collection.)

This is a waterfront view of the Grant Porter-Smith shipyard in 1919. During World War I, wooden-hulled ships were manufactured there for the US government. When the armistice was signed on November 11, 1918, operations ceased. (Author's collection.)

This c. 1918 photograph shows the Peninsula Shipbuilding Company's cutting-up plant. (Courtesy Gholston collection.)

Henry J. Kaiser's Oregon Shipbuilding Corporation was built along the Willamette River next to Terminal 4. This image was captured around 1944. Oregon Ship produced Liberty, Victory, and attack transport ships. (Courtesy Portland Archives, A 2004-002-6712.)

During World War II, shipyards labored into the night. This c. 1943 nocturnal view is of Oregon Ship. (Author's collection.)

This Christmas card shows the launch of the *Star of Oregon* from Oregon Ship in 1941. (Author's collection.)

A ship is seen just after its launch from Oregon Ship in the mid-1940s. (Author's collection.)

"New Apparel For Women Workers" was an article in a 1942 Kaiser Shipyards magazine, the *Bo's'n's Whistle*. It detailed the specific clothing available from local stores: "A fashion show was held after the launching of the SS *Gordon Charles Curtis* liberty ship. Six women from OSC were part of a fashion show to show off the latest shipyard attire for women." (Author's collection.)

Stubby Bilgebottom, cartoon character of the Kaiser Shipyards magazine *Bo's'n's Whistle*, is featured on this Oregon Ship ride share card. The instructions on the back of the card read: "Attach this card to your coat lapel with the paper clip. Stand facing Oregon Ship traffic in such a position that passenger car may see the card and identify you as an Oregon Ship employee wishing to obtain a ride. It is customary for riders to participate in the cost of operation of the driver's car. Pay your share of operation costs when due, be prompt in meeting your driver, don't abuse his car, share the ride, and conserve vital transportation for victory." (Author's collection.)

TRAINING MANUAL

Air Raid Warden Service

Portland-Multnomah County Civilian Defense Council

MAYOR EARL RILEY
Director

"Ask Your Block Warden . . . He Knows"

Elizabeth Rassi and Violet Jower were among the St. Johns residents who were air raid block wardens during World War II. They patrolled the streets to make sure that porch lights were off and curtains were closed. Even though women were block wardens, the cover betrays the prevailing attitude of the times: "Ask Your Block Warden . . . He Knows." Gilbert Noce kept watch of the St. Johns Bridge by binoculars. This training manual cover is from around 1943. (Author's collection.)

Vern L. Elser, a rigger at Oregon Shipyard Corporation, was formerly a logger. He is shown tending his garden at the St. Johns Parkside Homes development in 1943. This photograph appeared in the *Bo's'n's Whistle* magazine, which covered the activities of workers and the shipyards of Henry J. Kaiser in Portland and Vancouver, Washington. (Author's collection.)

This aerial view is of the Swan Island Shipyard, the former site of the Swan Island Airport, in 1943. A parking lot at left is connected to the island. (Author's collection.)

Swan Island Tanker Champs were a diverse mix of shipyard workers, as shown on the cover of this November 11, 1943, issue of the *Bo's'n's Whistle*. During World War II, 147 T-2 tankers were produced here. (Author's collection.)

Saundra Fleming, a Bluebird in the Camp Fire Girls organization, was a flower girl for the launch of the tanker ship SS *Camp Namanu* in 1944. Camp Namanu was a Girl Scout camp located along the Sandy River. (Courtesy Saundra Fleming Rassi.)

Shirley Nelson, Billie Johnson, and Elaine Nelson lean against a railing in North Portland's Peninsula Park around 1944. They worked at Columbia Aircraft during World War II, where they riveted rudders for PBY Catalina airplanes. (PB is for Patrol Bomber, and Y was the code assigned to Consolidated Aircraft.) (Author's collection.)

Eight

Swan and Hayden Islands

Swan Island, the site of the first boat-building venture of 1840, was developed as the Port of Portland Airport. Before it opened, a causeway was built to the island to connect it to the mainland; the airport opened in the mid-1920s. As airplanes increased in size, it became more difficult to land them here. A new airport was built in Northeast Portland and opened in 1940. The main channel of the Willamette River went between Swan Island and the Mock's Bottom wetlands before 1926. This c. 1902 photograph shows a steamboat helping a steamship navigate the channel. Swan Island is covered with water. (Author's collection.)

Mock's Bottom, a wetland that was used for duck hunting, is seen in this c. 1900 photograph. At center left is Methodist University, which within one or two years would be sold and become the Catholic Columbia University, today's University of Portland. (Author's collection.)

Spectators watch from railroad tracks toward Mock's Bottom as airplanes are being readied for a Victory Loan air show event in 1919. US, French, English, and German biplanes that were captured by the Allied forces performed aeronautical feats. (Author's collection.)

An American Eagle airplane named *Wings of the Morning* was used by the Apostolic Faith Church in Portland to deliver printed materials from their headquarters to affiliated churches. The airplane was also used for transportation of ministers to churches they were assigned to. This 1929 photograph shows the plane at the Port of Portland's Swan Island Airport. (Author's collection.)

An airplane takes off from the Swan Island Airport in 1933. Aviator Charles A. Lindbergh visited Portland in September 1927 advocating for passenger air travel. He landed his *Spirit of St. Louis* at Swan Island Airport. (Author's collection.)

This United Airlines plane, a Mainliner DC-3, is being refueled at Swan Island Airport around 1939. The aircraft was manufactured by Douglas Aircraft Company. (Author's collection.)

This is a c. 1939 view of the observation deck at Swan Island Airport, where visitors could get an up-close view of arriving and departing aircraft. (Author's collection.)

Hayden Island, south of the Columbia River and north of the Columbia Slough, was projected as a possible site for a 1925 world's fair, the Atlantic-Pacific Highways & Electric World Exposition. The East Side Business Men's Club was a strong advocate for it, according to a 1921 proposal. Many locations around the state were proposed. After much exploration, and even the approval of the US government, the exposition never happened. This is an illustration of the proposed Hayden Island site. (Author's collection.)

This view of Hayden Island looks east during the 1948 flood. The Jantzen Beach amusement park is at center. (Author's collection.)

The Dipper roller coaster in this c. 1940 photograph, sometimes referred to as "the Big Dipper," entertained riders at Jantzen Beach Park for over 40 years. (Courtesy Stephen Kenney.)

This photograph from the late 1940s shows attractions on the Promenade at Jantzen Beach Park. The beloved carousel at right is among the rides. (Courtesy Stephen Kenney.)

Former major league baseball player Carl Mays opened a baseball school for young men in the mid-1930s. It was located at Jantzen Beach Park in North Portland. The illustration shows the ballpark. Mays played in the majors from 1915 to 1929. In 1920, he hit a batter in the head with a pitch, which killed the player. (Courtesy Dave Eskenazi.)

This photograph of Jantzen Beach Park during the 1948 flood also shows Waddle's restaurant at left center. (Author's collection.)

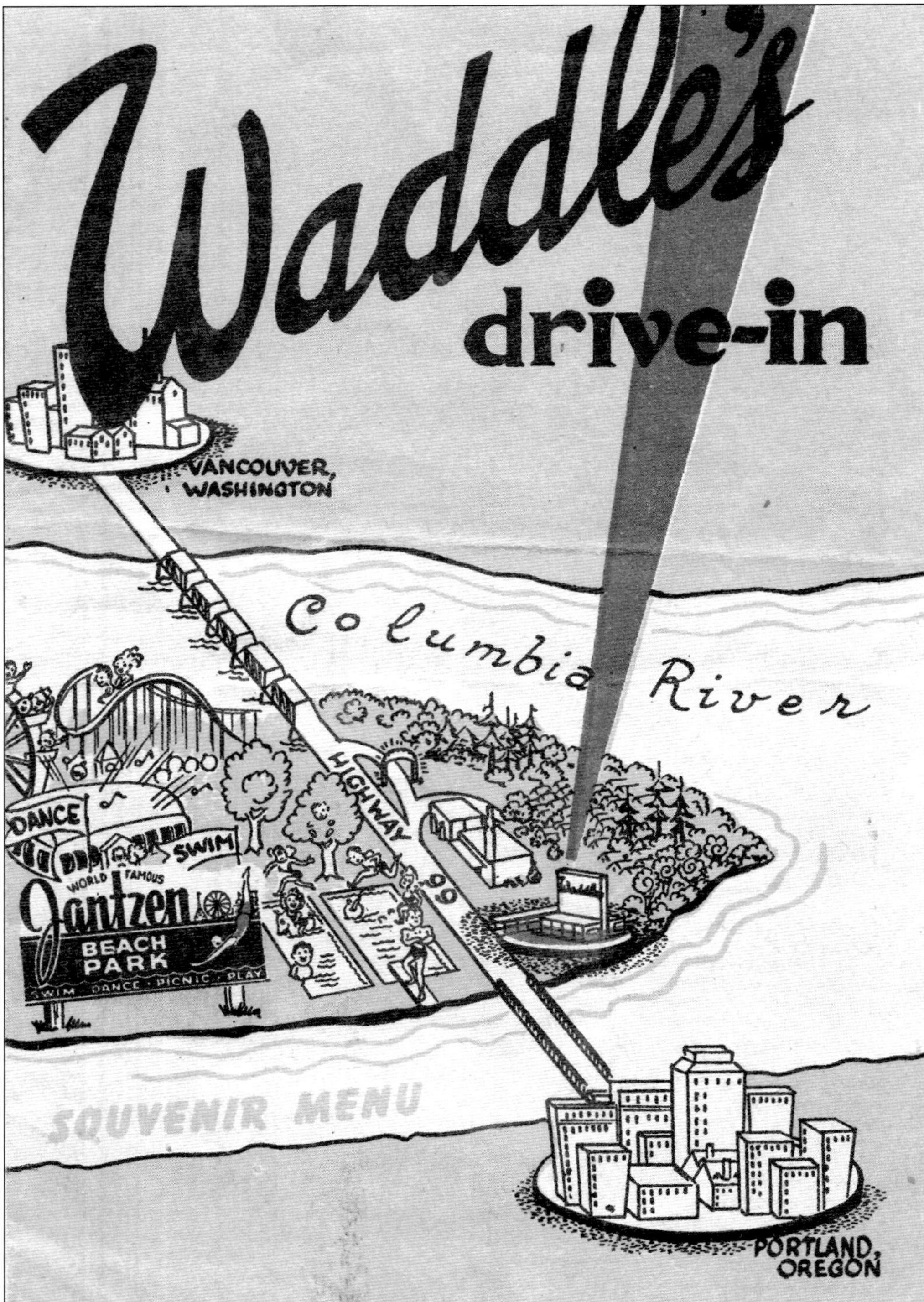

This 1940s souvenir menu for Waddle's shows the tip of Hayden Island. Jantzen Beach Park is on the left side of Highway 99, with Waddle's on the other side. (Author's collection.)

Nine

COMMUNITIES

Many neighborhoods were developed around St. Johns in the 1890s. University Park was named for the Methodist Portland University overlooking Swan Island. This 1890 view shows the Portsmouth area, which is near North Lombard Street and North Portsmouth Avenue. (Courtesy OHS, Org. Lot 1390.)

The original Portsmouth School faced North Hereford Avenue; the back of the building faced Gloucester Avenue, and it was north of Lombard Street. This view shows the front and side of the building. The original structure was erected in 1894; additions were built in 1903, 1907, and 1910. The old school was torn down in 1928. (Author's collection.)

The image shows the side and back of the school. A new school was built at another location in 1927. (Author's collection.)

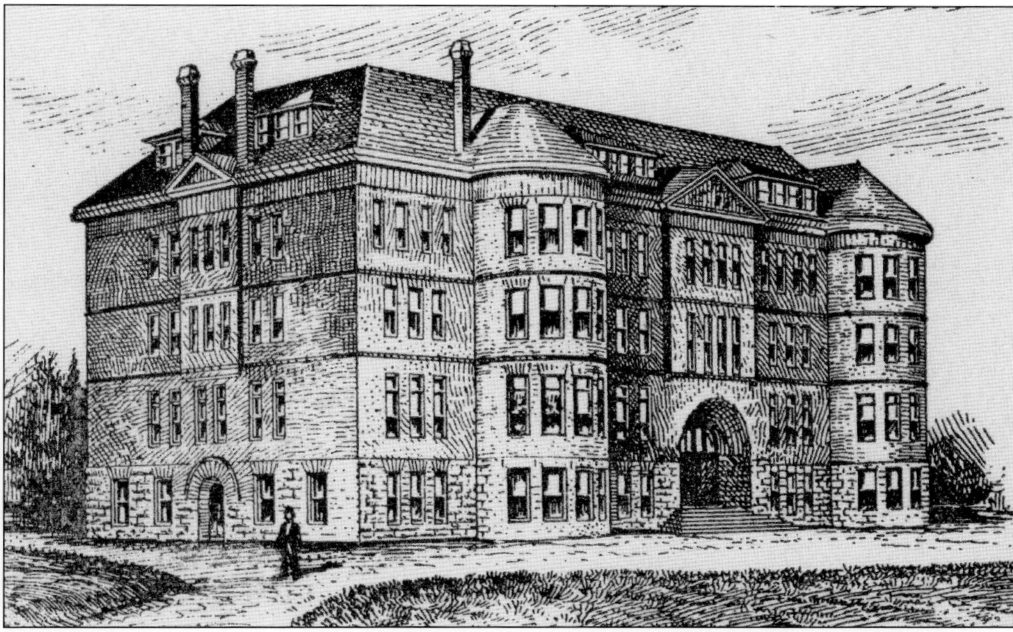

Portland University's West Hall was erected in 1891. The university closed in 1898. The property of the university was purchased by Archbishop Alexander Christie in 1901, who opened a Catholic school on the property, which is known today as the University of Portland. This building is now known as Waldschmidt Hall. This is an 1894 etching. (Author's collection.)

Many parts of Portland were lobbying to host the Lewis & Clark Centennial Exposition in 1905. This mural, painted in 1901 by Ernest Miller, founder of Miller Paint, depicts what was envisioned for the proposed University Park site. The dark structure at left center later became the University of Portland. (Author's collection.)

This is an aerial view of the University of Portland in 1919. Willamette Boulevard is visible at upper left. (Courtesy Bud Clark and Mike Ryerson collection.)

Vince "Pesky" Paveskovich warms up while University of Portland baseball coach Jack Wilson watches. Wilson, a former student when it was named Columbia University, played for the Boston Red Sox for several years. Paveskovich, an aspiring baseball player, graduated in 1948 and received his master's degree in 1956. He was among the first teachers at Marshall High School in 1960 and later was a disciplinary administrator. Today, he is admired among his former students. (Author's collection.)

Pioneer John Mock, who came to Portland in the 1860s, built his home on North Willamette Boulevard in the 1890s. His two previous log homes had burned down. Mock was a farmer; he owned over 450 acres of land, including the industrial area that earlier was on the main channel of the Willamette River known as Mock's Bottom. The image below was captured around 1868. (Above, photograph by author; below, courtesy T.J. Nealond's descendants.)

The University Park Methodist Episcopal Church, seen in this c. 1910 image, was located at North Fiske Avenue and North Lombard Street. (Courtesy Stephen Kenney.)

The office building at lower left in this c. 1908 photograph is still in use today. In the foreground is North Lombard Street; North Fiske Street angles up from lower right. (Courtesy Gholston collection.)

This is the University Park Baptist Church at North Fiske Avenue and North Drew Street around 1910. Today, it is St. Paul Missionary Baptist Church. (Courtesy Stephen Kenney.)

This is painter Charles H. Matson's house on North Drew Street around 1910. Their horse Babe stands in front. Matson's son Cecil would occasionally sleep on the sleeping porch off his second-story bedroom. (Courtesy Mary O'Donnell.)

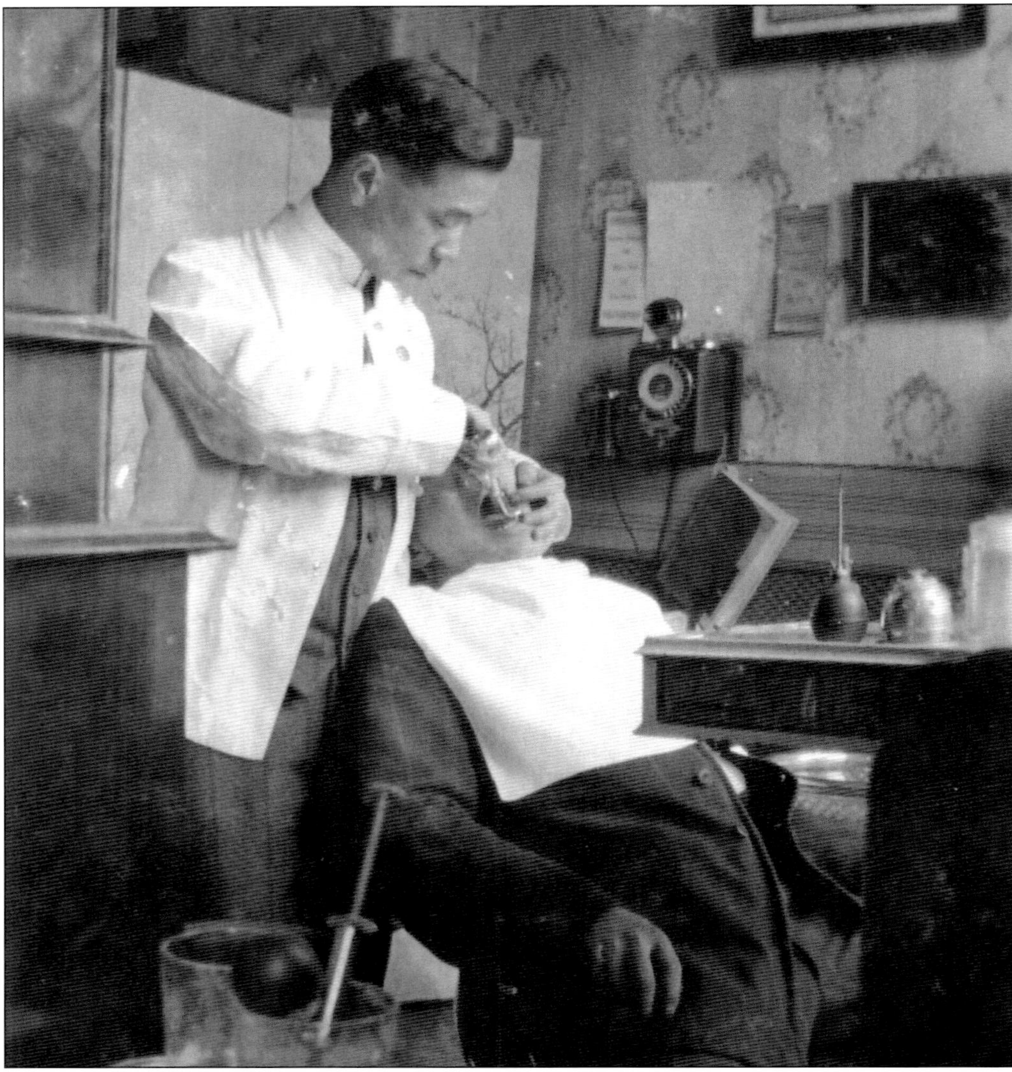

Dentist Masahiro Oyamada is seen in his first office in 1918 in Northwest Portland. He was a well-known dentist and fisherman during the 1920s and 30s. He, his wife, and two sons had to relocate to the Assembly Center at the Portland Stockyards in 1942 as a result of the government's exclusion order. It was a forced excluded community for those of Japanese ancestry, who were then sent to various internment camps across the United States. It was used for over four months. Oyamada gave his observations about his family's quarters in his personal journal: "At the Evacuation [Assembly] Center-Beginning May 5th (1942). We got in sec[tion] 4-D-20 square place plywood wall, no nothing, 4 beds 4 matress, no water, no sink, no heat, no windows, no doors, no carpet. Felt funny-no more freedom, regulation this, regulation that, 10:30 lights out. Food is coarse. This is our home for how long? Maybe we can get used to, maybe not. Baby cried next apt. and not much sleep. Afternoon boys went to hospital and started to work." One year later, he wrote, "Anniversary-Relocation-Portland Center Assembly (Pig Pen) now little better here (Heart Mountain). (Courtesy D. Oyamada.)

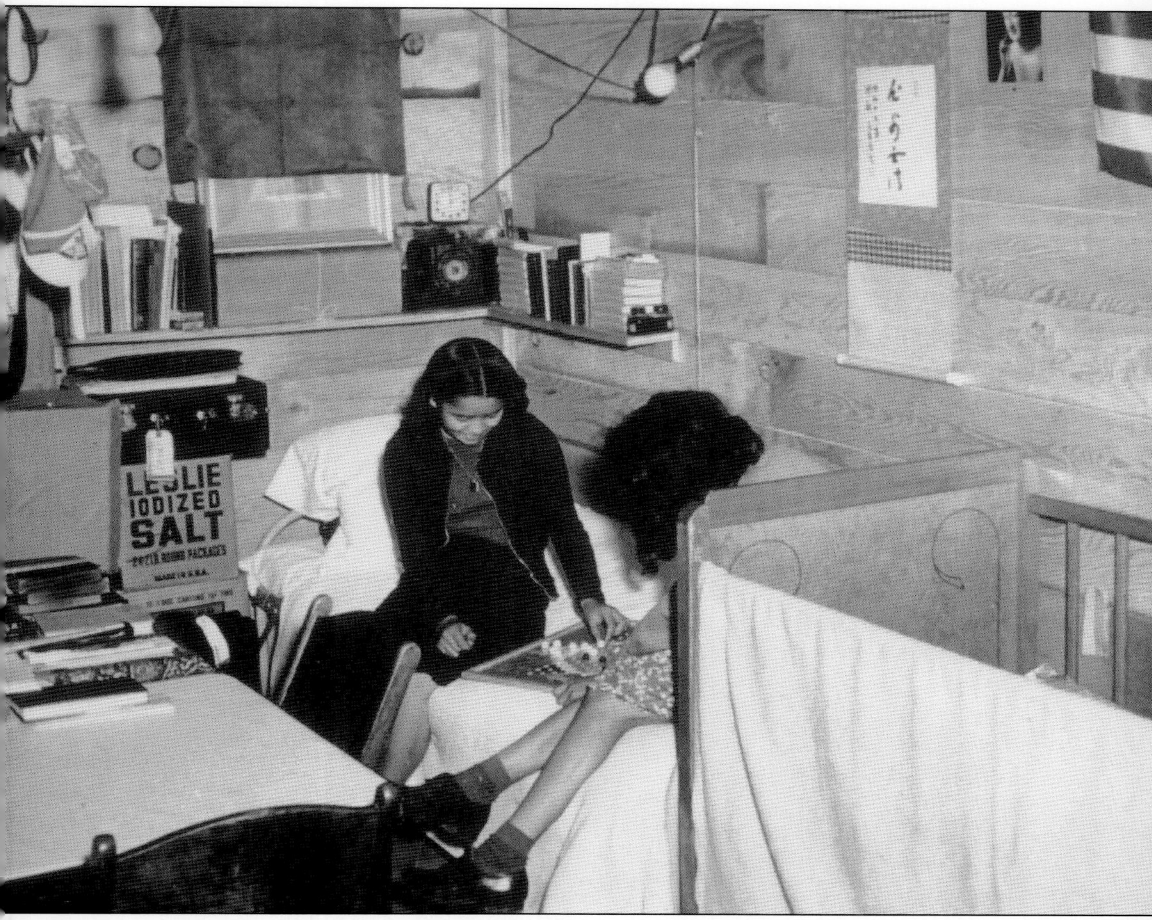

This is a view of one of the "apartments" of the detainees, which was built in the former animal stalls at the Portland International Livestock Pavilion show buildings. The caption for the photograph dated May 31, 1942, in the *Oregon Journal* read, "The Japanese live in Portland assembly center apartments inside Pacific International Livestock show buildings shown in this photo of the 5-person apartment of the Rev. T. Terakawa, a Buddhist priest. Playing Chinese checkers are the Rev. Terakawa's daughter, Hiroko Terakawa, and friend, Lillian Hayashi. The government furnishes steel cots and mattresses only, the Japanese evacuees the rest, including in this case American Flags, baby crib, small radio, books." (Used with the permission of the Oregonian Publishing Co., © Oregonian Publishing Co.)

In 1959, seventeen years after the Portland Assembly Center was closed, the Livestock Pavilion was transformed into the Oregon Centennial Exposition and International Trade Fair. (©Thomas Robinson.)

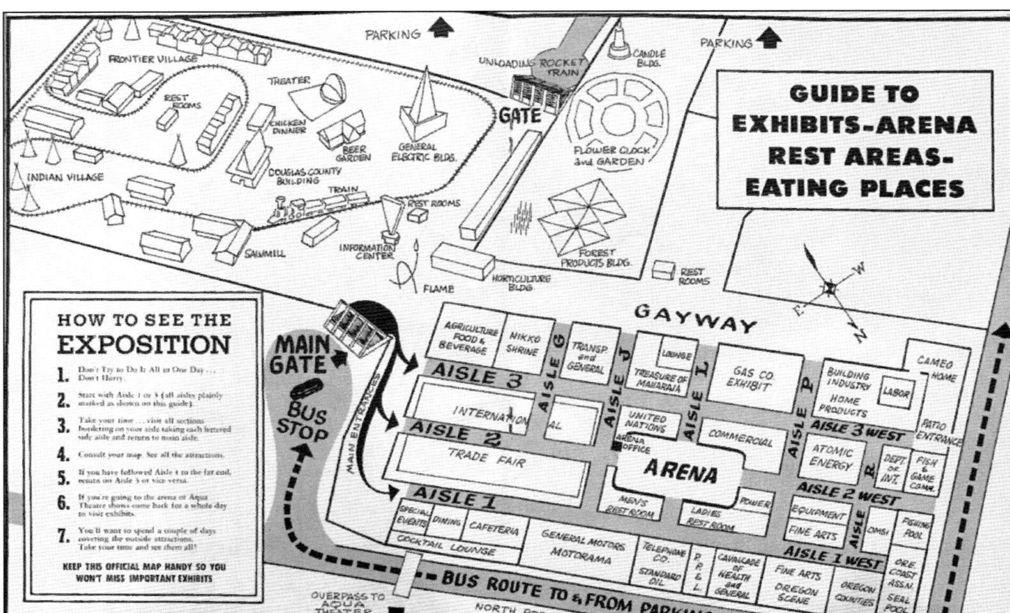

This map from a souvenir program for the centennial is a guide to the various buildings and areas. (Author's collection.)

The Zooliner, originally at the Washington Park Zoo, along with the steam train from the zoo railway, provided rides at the Oregon Centennial Exposition in 1959. (Author's collection.)

In 1965, the stockyards were acquired by Multnomah County and named the Multnomah County Exposition Center, where the Multnomah County Fair was held for nearly 30 years. Metro took it over in 1994 and renamed it the Metropolitan Exposition and Recreation Commission. It is known today as the Portland Expo Center. Trade shows and antique festivals are held at the facility. (Photograph by author.)

The Columbia Slough curves through this early 1940s view of Vanport City, a wartime housing project in North Portland that was devastated by a flood on May 30, 1948. The inscription on the back of the original photograph reads, "Vanport City in good ole days." (Author's collection.)

This view of Vanport City, also referred to as Vanport, is a pre-flood c. 1944 photograph. It looks southeast toward North Denver Avenue. (Author's collection.)

Vanport was a mixed-race segregated community. In this 1948 photograph, residents with suitcases in hand head toward higher ground after the dike broke. (Author's collection.)

Bob and Shirley Korsmyer and their infant son Gary lived in the Vanport war housing development. The night before the flood, Bob, concerned about his wife's and son's safety, envisioned them trying to escape the floodwater while he worked. After work, he took them to stay with relatives in McMinnville. When he went back to their apartment house to retrieve belongings the next day (May 30, 1948), the dike broke, and he hurriedly escaped the flooding in his pickup truck. This photograph is from late 1947. (Author's collection.)

Young Victor Shackleton was near Westerlund's Moorage during the high water of the Columbia in May 1948, near the bridge to Jantzen Beach. According to him, they heard that the dike at Vanport broke and saw waves of water coming again and again, 100 yards apart. (Author's collection.)

Vanport College, located within Vanport City, was but two years old when the railroad dike broke. John F. Cramer (dean of the college) and Stephen Epler (president) went into action just before the flood. A news account quoted Cramer: "He said all records and most of the office equipment at Vanport College were salvaged. Sensing trouble, Cramer and Epler loaded the school records and most office equipment on a truck and were pulling away from the building when the dike broke through." (Author's collection.)

Portland International Raceway and Heron Lakes Golf Course were built on the former site of Vanport. (Photograph by author.)

These are some of the artifacts from the Vanport flood found in the mud by Vanport archeologist T.J. (Photograph by author.)